Hannah's Prayer

A devotional for women experiencing infertility + desiring to birth greatness

By Brittney Holmes Jackson

Hannah's Prayer

A devotional for women experiencing infertility + desiring to birth greatness

By Brittney Holmes Jackson

Copyright © 2021 Brittney Holmes Jackson & Co.

All rights reserved. This book or any portion thereof may not be reproduced or used in any manner whatsoever without the express written permission of the publisher except for the use of brief quotations in critical articles or book review. *For permission requests, contact* Brittney Holmes Jackson at contact@brittneyholmesjackson.com.

Printed in the United States of America

First Printing, 2020

ISBN 978-1-7359807-3-7

Publisher: Brittney Holmes Jackson & Co.
Stonecrest, GA 30038
www.BrittneyHolmesJackson.com

Dedication

For every woman who has felt an empty womb and experienced an unanswered prayer

Acknowledgements

First and foremost, I always honor my Lord and Savior, Jesus Christ. Without Him, I could not walk in purpose the way I am today. Thank you for pressing pause on my plans to ensure I prioritized Yours above all else.

Husbae, bae, I don't know what I would do without your support and encouragement. You are my quiet hype man, always rooting for me and boosting me up way past my personal confidence level. I appreciate how much you admire my drive, which is highly influenced by you. Thank you for giving me the space, support, prayer and all other things I needed to do this work.

To my parents, Drs. Michael and Kendra Holmes, thank you for your pastoral leadership and encouraging my spiritual growth beyond levels I would be comfortable with on my own. Your guidance has allowed me to pursue my purpose more wholeheartedly than ever before.

To my parents-in-love, Reverend Jerome and Elder Connell Jackson. I do not believe I could have asked for a better second set of parents. Mom, you are partly the inspiration for this book and you all's prayers and words of encouragement over Chris and I are invaluable. Thank you for loving me like your own.

Crystal, siiiiissstttaaahhh! You show me daily what it means to be a god-fearing wife and mother. Who would have thought that the youngest would become the wisest? You've taught me a lot on this journey to motherhood, whether you realize it or not, and I love and appreciate you for it.

Shoutout to my Hannah's tribe: Alexandria, Erica M, Faith, Ashley, Vernique, Cici, Tanesha, Bridgette, Loretta, Stephanie, Tamika, Jeida. Y'all prayed, cried, prophesied, and covered me over the past couple of years as I have fought the emotional battle of conception. Your words of wisdom, your moments of truth, your offerings of vulnerability, and so much more extended beyond the "requirements" of friendship. Your sisterhood has literally been everything for me.

Supernatural Childbirth Facebook group, we have shared many moments of sadness, praise, prayer and frustration. I appreciate you all for being a safe space, for believing God on my behalf and for sowing into this book, whether you submitted a testimony to be featured or you supported the overall publication process. I pray God's will includes giving you the desires of your hearts, in the form of children.

CJ, Carissa, and the rest of the unnamed Jackson clan, please know that your mother and father prayed incessantly for you, and we are excited to begin welcoming you into our family. Our foundation is strong, and the legacy being established is rich. I pray you each arrive healthy and whole, and that God is glorified through your earthly existence. I cannot wait to meet you.

Readers, especially those desiring to become mothers, your time is coming. God has not forgotten you and I hope that the pages of this book help you remember that. When things get rough and it seems like your prayers are being unheard, remember Hannah's story (and that of other barren women in the Bible), and know that God is in control.

October 14, 2020

Heavenly Father,

    You know my deep desire for a child. A little one to love and to hold, to care for, to cherish. Grant that my body may conceive and give birth to a beautiful, healthy baby in Your holy image. Guide me in all my choices so that this conception, my pregnancy and my baby's birth are in line with Your will. Heavenly Father, hear this prayer of my heart, mind and spirit.

Amen

Introduction

I just liked about five or six photos of babies posted by my family and friends on Facebook.

So pretty!

Aww, they definitely had the same baby twice.

My goodness, she's adorable.

Ooooohhh, my baby boy will be this handsome.

These were the only thoughts that rushed through my mind and not once did I feel an ounce of envy. I know it seems like it should be normal to ogle over the beauty of childbirth and infancy, however, my struggles to get pregnant had at one point and time left me frustrated at the sight of a baby picture or announcement on social media. Crazy, right? But up until recently, it had been my reality.

You see, at 30 years old and married for over five years, I felt as if I should have had not one, but multiple children by now. If I'd had my way, I would've gotten married and given birth to all of my offspring by the age of 25...27 at the very latest. Yes! I know, I was living in the 1980s because I was trying to mimic the life I had known my mother, aunts and grandmothers to live. By the age of 22, my mother had been found by and married her soul mate. At 23, they gave birth to their greatest joy and gift – ME – followed 3 years later by my baby sister, who is almost equally as great. Seriously though, married and two children by 26 was the standard for me and again, 30 had graced me with its presence and marriage had been the only thing I'd "achieved," and even that was "late" by about 4 years.

With my younger sister having had two baby girls and ironically being 3 years my junior, she had been blessed with the life of motherhood I'd prayed for myself. When people would ask me when we planned to have children, my answer was always, "Hopefully soon. We're not doing anything to prevent it." Eventually, it got to the point where the questions of "when" were starting to wane because my parents, in-laws, and extended family realized that this was a sore topic for me.

Instead of questions, prayers and spiritual intercession began. It was empowering and humbling, yet nearly humiliating at the same time. Why did I need prayer just to get pregnant? It didn't seem like something other women were doing … they were simply popping children out like toast, in my cynical opinion. But the power of prayer gave me hope, especially when it was coming from proven anointed vessels. However, even at the start of the draft of this book, I was in the midst of dealing with the emotional turmoil that came courtesy of Aunt Flow's severely late arrival. As a woman with a super regular cycle, anything past 3 or 4 days late is a pregnancy scare. So, when that exact thing began to happen during the cycles in which my husband and I were actually trying, my hopes were so high that when Flow would eventually arrive, they crashed so hard, it took several days to piece them back together so that I could get the faith up to try again.

      The idea to create a devotional for women TTC (the social acronym for "trying to conceive") honestly came in the midst of my overcoming and wanting others to not experience the intense myriad of emotions that I did even while penning this work. Literally, these words were written hours after I'd spent half of the day in bed, crying over the fact that I'd gotten my period 5 days late. So, I can't even pretend as if I wrote this *after* overcoming. This devotion was definitely written while in the midst of the storm. This devotion was written for me. I hope it provides you with all it has given me during this journey to motherhood.

Make Your Requests Known

"'O Lord of Heaven's Armies, if you will look upon my sorrow and answer my prayer and give me a son, then I will give him back to you.'"

1 Samuel 1:11 NLT

Asking God for things seems like such an exhausted concept. We've likely been asking God for anything and everything since we were old enough to say grace over our food, asking that He keep anything unclean off of our plates and out of our systems. In childhood, we kneel before our beds at night and ask God to protect our mommy, daddy, siblings, pets, other family members, and inanimate toys we had personified as human. We ask Him to forgive our sins and to get our schoolyard enemy back for taking our spot in line. We beg Him to force our parents to buy us toys that we grow tired of after a few weeks. Our prayers are so fervent because we *believe* we deserve what we are asking for and we have *faith* that God will hear us and oblige.

Interestingly enough, as we grow older, that belief and faith in God's favor wanes.

Maybe we have experienced the loss of a loved one to an illness we passionately prayed away. Or we might have prayed for a reprieve on our job for years, only to still be stuck in the same position with the same stressors from the same people. It's normal to become hesitant to ask God for anything after experiencing disappointment in not receiving what we have previously asked for. If we aren't mature enough in our Christian walk, it is often hard to accept the idea that maybe God's "no" or "not right now" is a form of protection or even preparation for something better. Whatever the reason, we have grown to second guess seeking God with our desires, and this is not the moment to do so.

Now is the time to tell God exactly what you want. Make your request known to Him (Philippians 4:6) without reservation. As I write these words, I am recovering from another bout with depression and feigned nonchalant feelings of still not being pregnant. The introduction of this book and this first section are literally months apart, page count not even a factor. This journey of asking is one that comes with a sacrifice of self that I was not willing to give.

When I initially began to ask and pray, seeking God for a child, it was at the encouragement of my mother-in-law, who outright asked me if we wanted children. I was not in the habit of sharing personal feelings or emotions with her, or anyone else for that matter. She was never a person I wanted to go to for any "issues" in my marriage. I am the wife of her baby boy, whom she still dots on often, not to my dismay at all. While I tease my husband for being spoiled, he's honestly blessed to have parents who are still able to show favor toward him, and ultimately me. That was something to get used to as an independent young woman who had often taken care of the others around her.

My first real conversation with my mother-in-law about children allowed me to open up about the fact that I didn't feel like I needed to ask God for children because He knows. He knows!!! I've wanted children since adolescence ... you just read that I had the whole motherhood timeline planned out. Imani and Isaiah (my hopefully twin baby names) should be preparing to start school right about now. It was almost empathetic, or maybe full of pity, when she looked at me and said, "Brittney," in only the way she can say my name, "Noooo, that's not how that works." I was fighting off tears. I didn't even know they were there until she asked me why I was crying. Then I just poured out. I was over it. Why do I have to ask God for something He knows has been my heart's desire for my entire life?

Then she told me to read Hannah's story and pray her prayer.

I sighed and replied, "Okay." The sigh was from the fact that I had grown up in church. I know Hannah, Ruth, Esther, all the ladies ... well, most of the women in the Bible. I know she prayed for a son and then eventually got one. Isn't that what I was already doing? My hopes were prayers. That was my rationale. However, going home that same weekend and reading 1 Samuel changed my entire perspective on what praying and making your request known to God really meant. So, I really studied Hannah's prayer.

As a brief overview, Hannah was one of two wives of a man named Elkanah, and while his other wife, Peninnah had been able to conceive multiple times, Hannah had struggled. She felt worthless, though her husband valued her immensely, giving to her more than he gave to his other wife. Interestingly enough, Hannah was nearly alone in her frustration because Elkanah cherished her so much more than anything that her being barren was not a dealbreaker. He even asked her at one point, "Am I not better to you than 10 sons?" (vs. 8). I often laugh when reading that because it sounds just like a man. My husband never said anything like this, but he surely made me feel like children

HANNAH'S PRAYER

weren't that important. I now know he simply was trusting God's timing, and we'll get to that later.

But Hannah wasn't happy with just her husband, and to make matters worse, Peninnah was trash! She would tease Hannah and flaunt her ability to conceive, causing Hannah to feel insecure. Was it not enough that her husband needed two wives (my personal modern-day opinion), but of the wives, she was the one to struggle with conception? Talk about a complete TKO. She honestly wasn't winning in any area, but God favored her, and she knew that if she sought Him, she would receive an answer for her prayers.

She went to the temple and cried ... I mean cried, telling God that if He would give her a son, she would return the child back to God, vowing to never cut his hair. Refraining from hair cutting in this day and age, specifically for the Nazirite, was a symbol of being completely devoted to the Lord. The priest Elijah thought she was a wino and nearly condemned her for being drunk in the temple. But she confessed her faith to him, and he blessed her, further solidifying her prayer. She went away and the next day lay with her husband and eventually conceived her son, Samuel.

Now, this is not the end of Hannah's story. It's the exact opposite, serving as the beginning of her overflow of blessings from God, but we have to know that making our requests known should not be left up for God's interpretation. The idea here is that, yes, He knows what we desire, but He wants us to commune with Him, spend time talking to Him about our desires, ensuring they align with His for our lives, and understand that His timing is perfect.

Communing with God is something many of us would hardly do if we didn't need something from Him, myself included. When our lives are going well, we often overlook devotions, prayers, and meditation time with our deserving Father. Someone on the outside looking in might even say that Christians have to go through turmoil to even seek God's face for any length of time. Take a look at how the world responds when in crisis. It's not a statement intended for criticizing, but for reflecting. God may be holding out on us for many reasons – timing, sanctification, or preparation to consider a few. But ponder on the idea that He could possibly just want you to directly ask Him.

Now I'm not saying God is toying with you or your emotions to get you to have a conversation with Him. His word literally tells us to "ask and keep on asking" (Matthew 7:7, AMP). So why are we so hesitant to do so? It's a level of selfishness and fear. We don't want to get *our*

HANNAH'S PRAYER

hopes up. We don't want to wait if it's not on *our* time. But we can't get tired of trying. Similar to a child who will nag his parents for a toy or food until they are granted their request, we have to constantly be in God's presence, letting Him know our desires until His answer is clear.

So, I took my mother-in-law's advice and began praying for my child(ren), letting God know how desperately I desired to have them. What I didn't expect was a different type of birthing though. As I was praying for purpose to be birthed in my womb, clarity in my spiritual purpose was being conceived. Another topic we will dive into shortly, but as you navigate this devotion, understand that while we are asking God for one thing, He may be asking us to get in position for another.

REFLECTION

Take a pause here and consider your request. What are you seeking God for? A child? Clarity in your call? Rest? Manifestation of other desires? Jot it in this space in whatever way your creativity and heart are best expressed.

Children ARE A GIFT FROM THE *Lord;* THEY ARE A *reward* FROM HIM.

PSALMS 127:3 NLT

Are You Aligned?

"Hannah was in deep anguish, crying bitterly as she prayed to the Lord. And she made this vow: "... He will be yours for his entire lifetime, and as a sign that he has been dedicated to the Lord, his hair will never be cut."

1 Samuel 1:10-11 NLT

Oftentimes, we ask God for our hearts' deepest desires and when they don't come to pass, we wonder if God is even real. Does He hear us? Does He care? Is His will even for us to have children? If it is, then why not now? If not now, when?

I just knew it would be my life's mission and purpose fulfilled to be a young mother with a house full of children running around ... taking joy in yelling for them to "stop all that noise before I come up there!" I chuckle at the thought now. Even thinking about it at this moment, I'm somber and also humbled. My plans clearly were never aligned with God's. And that sucks!

Praying for something ... anything to happen is a risk. We often take that risk and misapply our faith to make us believe that

HANNAH'S PRAYER

because we are children of God, we are *entitled* to receive our desires, (read carefully) in the way that *we* want. When prayers aren't answered according to our desires or if God answers the prayer but in HIS WAY versus ours, we begin to waiver in our faith.

The reality is, if we go into prayer, not just making our requests known, but also asking for our desires to align with God's or simply understanding that the outcome will be HIS WILL alone, we wouldn't be so disappointed when things *seem* to not work out the way we want. It's truly something to ponder.

I get it. We want to believe that what we want, God also wants for us and in some cases, that's an absolute truth. It even says in His Word that "He gives the barren woman a home, making her a joyous mother of children" (Psalm 113: 9 NLT)! God's Word promises that the childless will have a plethora of offspring and not in dismay, but in exuberant joy! How amazing is that? God's promises are always "yes" and "amen." But it's so hard to remember that when our timeline is not in alignment with His.

What does that even mean?

First and foremost, God does not abide by the time laws that restrict us here on Earth. With that knowledge, a timeline should not even exist for us when we are seeking God for anything, whether it be children, a job, a husband, a home, or even something as complex as healing in our bodies. His purpose and will for our lives supersede anything we may ask of Him with our fleshly being. That simply means that if you are struggling to give birth, it could be that He has something more important for you to focus on in this season. Your struggle to give physical birth may be because God is positioning you for a metaphorical birthing process that is more aligned with the purpose to which you've been called.

Imagine this: Being so focused on the desire to have a child that you miss an opportunity to birth God's ultimate plan for your life. Because you are so focused on your timeline of events and your desires, you overlook a chance to manifest something greater for His kingdom and His glory. Talk about a heart check! This was and sometimes still is me.

Had I given birth to a child at the age that I'd planned, it is very unlikely that I would have found myself positioned to walk the purpose-driven life I am now journeying. Nothing about what I am currently doing, even in writing this book, is about me. Having a child would have been all about me, though I'm sure that would've changed as soon as the baby was

HANNAH'S PRAYER

born because those tiny beings are selfish without even understanding what that concept means. And they can't help it; they need every ounce of you, so much so that there's hardly anything else left to give anyone else, yourself and God included. And while that's not a statement to deter you from desiring children, it is one that requires reflection.

How does my misalignment hold me back from pursuing what God has actually called for me to pursue? What am I missing out on because I'm so focused on this one thing? Even more gut-wrenching, what is my misalignment and disobedience to God's voice costing me? What would it mean to have the child I most desire and be so far away from God that my spirit remains unfulfilled?

Even now, I find myself saying I'd give it all up for a son (or even a daughter) – there go those personal desires again. They never go away; it is up to us to make a conscious decision to allow God to do this work through us. Whether baby or business, pregnancy or purpose ... all of it belongs to Him. Not us. Hannah's alignment is what got her to where she wanted to be. She told God that if He just gave her a son, she would dedicate that child back to Him for all his days – symbolically demonstrated with the vow to never cut his locks.

Had she been misaligned, whether in her timeline or intentions for having a child, she may have experienced a longer wait as well. You see, while having children does glorify God and expand His kingdom, if it occurs while we are so far from Him, what does that mean for our children. How can we dedicate offspring to Him when we have yet to fully give ourselves over to His will?

It took me a very long time to get to this understanding. God and I were literally having conversations that sounded like me saying, "My way or the highway!" And God laughing or simply shaking His head. Sometimes He'd throw in a "I wish you'd trust Me." I'd love to insert a crying emoji here, but it was a constant battle that I knew I was not going to win and kept trying my hand at it anyway.

Hannah trusted God. She made her request known but had she not gotten her heart's desire until years after that prayer, do we believe she would have gone on and attempted to do things her way? Would she have left her husband? Would she have given up and told God where He can go and how He can get there? Let's be real as many of us have been there. I have and have had to repent because God has both my and my unborn children's interests at the center of His heart. Remember, before He formed us in our mothers' womb, He knew us (Jeremiah 1:5), and He also has plans for us, those that won't harm us but will allow us to benefit good things (Jeremiah 29:11). Why do we constantly work against these manifestations?

Okay so maybe you haven't realized that you're misaligned with God's desire for your life. Maybe you didn't know that you were placing Him on a timeline. So, let's really demonstrate what this looks like. If you find yourself constantly concerned with how old you are and how that aligns with what has occurred in your life up until this age, that is problematic. Yes, there is such a thing as a biological clock, but remember, God does not work on Earthly chrono. His time is not ours so while He has placed doctors and other scientists here to remind us how to live healthier lives and what our bodies may endure as they progress in age, God is the ultimate timekeeper and if He has promised you a child, age will not prevent that.

When you find that you are obsessed with monitoring your ovulation and experiencing grave emotional turmoil every month there are no signs or confirmation of pregnancy, you may be misaligned with God's purpose for your life. Of course, there are medical professionals who will tell us to monitor those things, but they shouldn't be consuming us to the point where we are in emotional distress when old Aunt Ruby makes her monthly rounds.

    Not too many months ago, when I was at the crux of my family planning journey, I began to do a ton of research, asking questions and joining social media groups focused on women TTC. I was super excited. I went and purchased an ovulation kit from Amazon. I ordered some Maca root to stimulate my body's fertility. I began taking prenatal supplements like candy daily. I just knew with all of this work I'd soon get my nine months of bloody relief.

    By month two of this routine, I was balled up, crying in the feminine aisle of Kroger because I was buying yet another box of tampons after declaring and decreeing that the last box would be just that ... THE LAST! It wasn't and hasn't been the last for a very long time. When I realized that the process of getting pregnant was overtaking me, ruining my chances of having an authentically intimate moment with my husband, and resulting in additional stress on my body as noted through unusually late periods and cramps with pain never before experienced, I had to fix it.

    While no issue presents itself with making our requests known to God, we must honor His omnipotence. We may ask, but the *"when we will receive"* part is totally up to Him. *"My thoughts are nothing like your thoughts," says the LORD. "And my ways are far beyond anything you could imagine"* (Isaiah 55:8 NLT). This scripture reminds us that once we align our focus with God's, we are able to experience the unthinkable, something greater than what we even have in mind for ourselves.

How do we do this? How do we get into alignment with God?

Relinquish your will.

The interesting thing about letting go of our personal will is the idea that when we think we have, we probably haven't. Relinquishing your will is a nicer way of telling someone to give up control, and most of us, especially as busy women who wear many hats, are unidentified control freaks. We like everything to be a certain way or done at a certain time. Seriously, ask our husbands how we might respond to missing a scheduled appointment, oversleeping, or an incomplete task. While the world doesn't literally end, it can be a difficult adjustment when we feel like things are out of our control and we do not have a hold on whatever situations we are facing.

Letting go of what we believe should be happening in our lives can be a consistent challenge. The idea is that if we give up control, then we have no idea how things will pan out. In reality, the issue isn't maintaining control; it's the lack of trust we have in the One who is actually in charge. As Christians, we have no control over the events and happenings of our lives. We can make all of the plans we want, but God's plans will always prevail. So many of us like to quote Jeremiah 29:11 (NLT), "For I know the plans I have for you, declares the Lord, plans for welfare and not for evil, to give you a future and a hope," as a means to provide encouragement for others. However, as soon as we need to apply this to our own lives, we tend to forget that God has already formed our futures as well. The Word also urges us to understand that He knew us before our formation and conception (Jeremiah 1: 5).

Our need for control undermines our ability to trust God and His plan for our lives. The moment we relinquish it, is the moment we tell God that we place all power in His hands. The biggest takeaway for me is that when we struggle with this, we minimize God's entity to that of a friend or stranger who we feel is not worthy of our trust. Imagine placing God on the same level as your average everyday person, someone who is fallible and innately has their own best interest at heart. To be clear, that is not a description of God. The best way to honor Him is to trust Him for Who He is.

Trust His timing and know that it is perfect.

If someone asked me what the most difficult part of this journey has been, I would have to say letting go of my timeline. It's one thing to trust God for Who He is, but it is another ballgame to be okay with His timing of events. My mom often says, "I can trust God like no one else. It's His timing that I struggle with!" Ironically, we have to ask ourselves, how much do we actually trust God if we don't trust every aspect of His will, which includes time.

There's a video from decades back, where a scientologist challenged a man of Apologetics, asking him the age-old question: Where did God come from? The answer is credited by Saint John's internet with being one of the best responses to this question of all time. The philosopher begins with a mic-drop statement of "[This question] displays that you're thinking of the wrong god, because the God of the Bible isn't affected by time, space, or matter." He honestly could have ended his response there, but he carries on, describing that God created time, space and matter, so He is, therefore, outside of these concepts. While receiving cheers from the audience, he concludes with "[This question is] assuming a limited god ... if I could fit the infinite God in my three-pound brain, He would not be worth worshiping!"

So first and foremost, I just want to be so in-tune with God that I can silence the naysayers and educate those with questions, but in addition to that, this is the argument I often have to think of when I consider God's timing. Lowkey, we shouldn't even call it His "timing" because it still insinuates that He abides by some numerical or measurable schedule, which He does not. We should simply label it God's will, which allows us to cycle this back to the idea of letting go of our will, including our own schedule and desires of time, and accepting God's plan in totality.

The second part of Jeremiah 29:11 reminds us that God only has positive blessings waiting for us. We are guaranteed a future and a hope. What does our future entail? What are we hoping for? The possible outcomes are endless, but, if nothing else, we know that it is not rooted in anything evil that would be harmful to us. It is imperative to believe that God, unlike others, prioritizes us. Ephesians 1, verses 10 and 11 tell us exactly what we need to know. "And this is the plan: At the right time He will bring everything together under the authority of Christ—everything in heaven and on earth. Furthermore, because we are united with Christ, we have received an inheritance from God, for He chose us in advance, and He makes everything work out according to His plan." All things will work together. Just trust Him.

Remain in communication with Him.

One of the best ways to achieve alignment with God's will is to talk to Him. The more we pray and focus on Him, we gain clarity and confidence in His plan and will for our lives. Though it sounds simple, we somehow find a way to avoid this part of the process, especially when we have been praying and praying, but not seeing the results we desire. It's a lot easier to evade communing with God when we aren't feeling Him in the moment. Remember this: FEELINGS ARE FLEETING! GOD IS UNCHANGING!

I am an advocate for allowing yourself to *feel* whatever you feel, even if it is in response to God. I've been known to advise friends to speak from the heart before shutting God out. The more negativity that we tend to experience, the further we tend to move away from God, and it is purely because we become silent. As a marriage and family therapist intern, I have come across clients who have stated they feel God has left them. By the time we get down to the root of the issue, we find that with each setback, with each let down, with each disappointment, they were spending less and less time with God. So when they believe that God is distant from them, it's because they are the ones to have created that distance.

When I'm mad, I talk to God. When I'm sad, I talk to God. When I'm disappointed, I talk to God. And let me be clear, this includes when I am mad AT God, sad BECAUSE of God, or disappointed IN God …. I know some would question the audacity to feel this way toward the Almighty, but these feelings are reflective of the events within an authentic relationship with Him, and instead of avoiding them or pretending they aren't felt, it is important to address them to allow the relationship to heal, grow and become whole. The point is, never close off your communication with God, even if that communication is laced with hurt, because that's when the distance occurs.

I won't pretend that this is an easy task. Just like giving up your will and trusting God's timing, this requires a level of vulnerability and trust that many of us are hesitant to display. Consider the flip side though. Not trusting and communicating with God doesn't get us anywhere either.

As you find your way back to communing with the Heavenly Father, ensure you're doing it in the most effective way possible, so those fleeting feelings don't deter you from consistency.

1. **Set a date with God.** We set dates with everyone else and for everything else. Why not make appointments to talk to God as well? If you know it's something you struggle with, it should be as intentional as a doctor's appointment or – let's be real, real – a hair appointment, because we aren't missing that!
2. **Establish a routine.** Create a recurring routine for this time so it's easier to stick with and you aren't going into the space without a plan and feeling as if it is a waste of time. A routine might look like: Going into your prayer space (a closet, an office, or simply your bedroom), starting with prayer, reading a scripture or devotional, and taking as little as five minutes to meditate on what God wants you to take from it, then closing by journaling and praying again. When finding a suitable scripture is difficult, using the verse of the day within the Bible app is always helpful or conducting a Google search for "scriptures about [insert current emotion or situation here]." Your routine is an outline;

always remain open enough to let God direct the time.

3. **Speak and feel freely.** Whether journaling, meditating or verbally praying, allow yourself to be open and honest during this time. Express gratitude first and foremost to ensure you are not neglecting the blessings God has bestowed upon you, then pour your heart out. Let Him know how you are feeling, why and what you hope for. Ask Him to guide you to the appropriate places in His Word that will remind you of His faithfulness and presence. Don't hold back!

4. **Incorporate worship.** Worship is simply allowing the atmosphere to transform into a place where God's presence can reside. You can set this using music or prayer. Welcoming God into the space, no matter how you are feeling toward Him, gives you an opportunity to *feel* Him. This is important for those of us that believe God is far away or unreachable during this season in our lives. Worship is literally an invitation for the Holy Spirit to reside with you. There's no way God would turn that down. Set the atmosphere.

REFLECTION

Take a moment to reflect on Matthew 6:33-34. What aspect of aligning with God's will are you most struggling with? How can this scripture be applied to help you overcome that struggle?

"Trusting the process hasn't been easy…"

My name is NeKesha Hill. I am a forty-three-year-old that was told at the tender age of sixteen that if I ever wanted to have children, I would have to take medication to make me ovulate. At sixteen I looked at my mom and asked, "Ma, what does that mean?" She began to tell me what it meant; however, it went in one ear and out the other. To be honest I was young, unmarried, and enjoying life at that time.

Life brings about a change. I got my life together and met my true love. I'm married now and we are ready to start our own family. We started trying on our wedding night, and nothing has happened yet. *What's going on here?* I'm not on any form of birth control. I've been to the doctor numerous times, and she always states, "You don't have any fibroid cysts and you're good." But make it clear, "NO I'm not!" She responds, "Mrs. Hill, just relax, enjoy the moment, and don't think about it."

I try not to, but at the end of the day I'm human. I don't have any biological kids and my husband has two. What's going on with me?! I'm just trying to continue to trust God and just

HANNAH'S PRAYER

patiently wait on my time. I will not give up, because God's promises are YES and AMEN! Trusting the process hasn't been easy, however it will be worth it when I have my own baby in my arms.

Signed patiently waiting,

Mrs. Hill

Just as you cannot understand the path of the wind or the mystery of a tiny *baby* growing in its mother's *womb*, so you cannot understand the activity of *God*, who does all things.

Ecclesiastes 11: 5 NLT

Worth More Than Ten Sons

> "Year after year it was the same—Peninnah would taunt Hannah as they went to the Tabernacle. Each time, Hannah would be reduced to tears and would not even eat. 'Why are you crying, Hannah?' Elkanah would ask. 'Why aren't you eating? Why be downhearted just because you have no children? You have me—isn't that better than having ten sons?'"
>
> 1 Samuel 1:7-8 NLT

My plans for having children never included my husband. I literally laugh out loud at that now, but the reality was, I had my pregnancy and birthing plan laid out before I even got married. Re-read the introduction. I should have been married with *all* my children by age 26. I didn't get married until I was 25. While that is still very young, God was not listening to any of my desires even back then, and, of course, now I understand that His plan was perfect. That didn't negate the plans I had in place. My husband was simply a necessary part of the equation. While I know there are many women who feel this way, as it's the "natural order" of the world, this was not the way to consider the man I had spent many years, even in my adolescence, praying for.

The issue was that this minimized my husband to being a sperm donor and if that's all I wanted, then I could go to the clinic for that. This man was literally a Godsend, especially considering all I had gone through in previous relationships, mostly voluntarily because of my gross immaturity and egregious pursuit of companionship and acceptance from the male species. I could get into all of that, and how it stemmed from my unresolved grief over losing my father at a young age, but that ain't what this is about. A husband is held to a seemingly higher standard in the marriage than the wife and his role extends far beyond planting seeds. Being called to love your wife just as God loves us as the body of Christ can be a challenge enough but having to do that when your wife struggles to honor you as more than a seed sower can be debilitating.

When reading Hannah's prayer, I felt the conviction in my own spirit. Elkanah's question of being better than ten sons received an immediate, "Nah, negro!" from me. While I initially said it in jest, I had to truly examine my heart concerning this. Because what if ... what if, God's plan was not for my husband and I to have children, biologically or otherwise? What if it were

His will for us to submit and sacrifice for the Gospel of Jesus Christ, to engage in missionary work, to travel and speak to the masses, which may not involve children? Now this is a huge "what if," but if it were not simply hypothetical, would my husband be enough?

See, the issue here is that many couples that do have children get so invested in their offspring's' lives that they neglect to nurture their marital relationship. The priority becomes football games, afterschool meetings, doctor's appointments, dance recitals, play dates, real dates and the like. Very little time is placed in romantic date nights, genuine and much-needed conversations, or even physical intimacy. I have especially seen mothers become so wrapped up in their children that they not only fail to respond to the needs of their husband, but they also tend to lose themselves and forgo attending to their own needs as well.

The question here is: What good will these children be if you have to raise them alone or can't raise them at all?

Yeah, I know ... cuss me out in your head or out loud. I swear I wouldn't ask you anything that I haven't had to address myself. There was a moment on this journey where I told my husband that if we weren't going to have children, then I did not want sex. Like, who raised me? I couldn't have been mad had he packed up his stuff that day and chucked the deuces on his way out of the door. The reality was that deep down in my heart, I knew my husband was not worth more than ten sons to me and I was blatantly treating him as if he wasn't even worth more than the one I was praying for. Even worse, I was choosing to not show love to my husband in the one way he needed, based on his identified love language.

    I often wonder how we, as women, deliberately elect to withhold our bodies from our husbands. Whether with malicious or selfish intent, we find ourselves giving ultimatums and wondering why we face other issues in our relationships. While everything we do should not be to simply keep a smile on our husband's faces, it is pretty selfish to neglect physical intimacy as a means to compensate for the voids amid our personal desires. What do we believe this will actually solve? How do we rationalize the idea that this is going to make our husbands do whatever it is we believe they should be doing? If nothing else, it worsens an already sensitive issue.

    In some cases, this becomes a biological challenge that is difficult to navigate. That was the case for me, anyway. I genuinely did not want to have sex if it was not an act that would immediately produce offspring. The interesting

HANNAH'S PRAYER

thing about physical ailments and deficiencies is that oftentimes, they start in the mind. Now I'm not speaking on incurable conditions that are truly physical, but those that we conjure up in our minds to make ourselves believe we are incapable of performing a task due to a biological dysfunction that simply does not exist. For me, this looked like believing sex should result in a baby, and when it did not, I no longer wanted sex. My mind told my body that because it could not achieve this thing, it shouldn't engage in intercourse at all, resulting in a lowered sex drive.

    How often do we tell ourselves that because we are "incapable" of doing something that we should just stop trying, or even worse, not even enjoy the process of getting there? We seem to only work in order to get something, to benefit from the output, or to garner praise. What about working to simply enjoy the connection, the growth, the process …? There's a quote I came across online that reads, "The goal isn't just to get there, but to have fun along the way." Such a simple concept, but one we make complex because we only keep our eyes on the prize. And yes, doing so helps us stay focused and undeterred, but how much scenery - or better yet the creations of God - do we miss on our journey because we are only looking at the finish line?

Aside from the fact that sex should be a fun and exciting experience within a marriage, it is also an opportunity to learn, grow, and join with your husband. Some of the greatest levels of intimacy are experienced during this time, not simply for pleasure but for spiritual connection to further your commitment and knowing of one another. If it were only to be used for reproduction, there would be no need for there to be a commitment to any one person or to anyone at all. We would be reconciled to utilize clinics that identify quality physical and mental features of the male species and offer us a cup of his semen to simply implant with the hopes of birthing a child that holds essentially good traits.

Sex within marriage is beyond procreation. Matthew 19:6 reminds us that a man and wife are one flesh once joined together. Proverbs 5:19 encourages us to delight and intoxicate ourselves with each other. And Song of Solomon … well, the whole dang book reminds us that physical intimacy with our spouse is a force of worship to be reckoned with, so much so that this entire book of the Bible is dedicated to explaining how much one man appreciates his wife's body and how this wife seeks after her husband's touch and being.

HANNAH'S PRAYER

The point is, our desire to give birth cannot be so domineering that we neglect this type of closeness with our husband. He has to be worth more to us than ten sons ... even the one (boy or girl) we would give up anything for. [Insert your husband's name here] cannot be so disposable that we are willing to give up a love we prayed for in our youth, some of us in our adulthood, to receive simply because God's timing is making things seem a little off. If we treat our husbands like this now, what happens when children do come into the picture? Will they be prioritized over our spouses?

It's important to note that children eventually leave the nest. They grow up, establish lives of their own, connect with others, and sometimes barely call to say "hey" and let their parents know how they're doing. We, wives, have to still live with the men we neglected when God didn't give us what we wanted. We, wives, still have to have a relationship with the men we silently resented because we blamed them for not being able to produce children. We, wives, still have to love the men we emotionally bashed because we could not curse ourselves or the God we serve when the IVF treatments failed. There is absolutely no way we can treat our spouses like trash while we seemingly struggle through this journey to conceive and actually expect to produce purpose in the form of our children. God will not bless that, and if He, by chance, does, you're in for an even greater struggle once the children come. Men have to feel important and needed and prioritized. This journey isn't just about us.

I'm in many Facebook groups for women who are TTC (Remember: trying to conceive) and very few of them are spiritually centered and welcoming to men. Most of them focus on the woman, her journey, her struggle, her need for support. It is rare to find a group that supports men through this kind of issue, and if you find it, it could be challenging to even get a man to join it, especially if he is the reason for the fertility challenges. However, there is one group that I am in that is faith-based and open to men, if they desire to join. It's properly coined "Supernatural Conception Pregnancy & Birth," inspired by a book with a similar title, *Supernatural Childbirth* by Jackie Mize. The book focuses on the idea that we are not tied to the punishment God placed on Eve when He told her that her pregnancy would be painful due to her disobedience. *"Then he said to the woman, 'I will sharpen the pain of your pregnancy, and in pain you will give birth. And you will desire to control your husband, but he will rule over you.'"* (Genesis 3:16 NLT). Now I'm not going to even touch that last part and let some of us pretend that we actually are in control of our households...I wish I could insert a side eye right here. But essentially God punished Eve, not every woman after her, and this book (get it if you don't have it) empowers the women of God to reclaim the supernatural spirit that makes childbirth painless and uninhibited by challenges that seem normal. You know, the idea that we absolutely positively will experience labor pains, and even though we planned a natural childbirth at home, in the bathtub or pool with a midwife, we are going to absolutely positively need to be in a hospital with a doctor who is going to force us into C-section or demand we push after we've screamed for an Epidural that we said we would never take. Yeah, none of that has to happen. You don't have to miscarry, you don't have to produce a stillborn, you don't have to endure pain to produce a child. But that's not why I brought up this group ... just get the book after you finish reading this one.

The Supernatural Conception, Pregnancy & Birth group is one that is open to men and though there aren't many men in it, as it's a small group to begin with, which I love, there was a recent post by a man that helped me realize that women aren't the only one's suffering (whether in silence or not). Men are invested in this process as well. One of the men in this group created a post to encourage the majority of the audience, who are women, and he shared a lot of great information, but one thing he wrote really stood out to me. He noted, "...your husband wants it as bad as you do, even if he doesn't show it. Even when he doesn't want to talk about it. Pray for his heart in the season as y'all are praying for [your] child."

Now ... I know for a fact that I had not prayed for my husband's heart or his processing of this. Chris and I, lowkey, spent the majority of our years trying to conceive while holding different perspectives on the matter. If you ask me how long we have actually been trying to conceive while on the *same page*, it's only been about two years. I spent the three years before that trying to conceive on my own, without him, but with him, if you understand what I mean. Remember, I started this chapter saying that my husband was essentially a pawn in this game of childless chess. My plans were established before the love story of Chris and Brittney was ever imagined (or so I thought), so he was just along for the ride.

To me, Chris's nonchalant attitude about everything, but especially about children, made me feel as if he didn't care. We never really discussed our family plans prior to marriage, and it never came up in premarital counseling. I believe I assumed because he was from a large family that he wanted kids and wanted them quickly. But that was not the case because his focus was on becoming a doctor. His own dreams had been deferred for many years and whereas he thought he would have his M.D. prior to marrying anyone, that had not been the case. So, while I am praying and planning for Christopher Jr., he was hoping that CJ didn't arrive before he could financially provide for him (or her). I ain't care nothing about that ... my biological clock was my priority. This divided us without us even realizing it.

When I would cry about my cycle coming, he would simply pat me on the back and tell me it was okay. When I would "encourage" him to go get checked out at the doctor, he would tell me he would try to work it around his rotation schedule. When I would tell him, I wasn't interested in sex if it wouldn't produce children, he would tell me - in so many words - to not provoke the beast. I married a gentle giant. A Hulk trapped inside of a Bruce Banner. A non-confrontational but very absolute man. He wasn't one to selfishly challenge or give ultimatums to, so telling him how our sex life would or wouldn't be or constantly provoking him because of my emotional instability on this matter was never the move.

What did work was explaining how not having children at this point in my life was impacting me emotionally and mentally so he could better understand and empathize with me. It also helped to affirm him so he would know that his job as a father was not to solely provide our children with things, but to also pour into them, which he was more than capable of doing whether he had money in the bank or not. Having family members and other professionals remind him, and ultimately us, that we would never be "ready" for the cost of children, was also a benefit. Eventually, we came to be on one accord about our family planning, but there was still a ways to go. Praying for him as he navigated his own feelings on this journey was never in my purview. Again, this is a process for growth and development. Imagine if God had answered my prayers when I was being superiorly selfish and focused on just what I wanted? I might have a child but could be on the verge of being a single parent. But with this time and this delay (not denial), I have grown as a wife. My husband has matured spiritually. We have enhanced our communication. It has been for our good.

So how do we avoid ostracizing our husbands when a child seems to be all we desire? How do we remember that our men are also a part of this process and in need of just as much support as us, maybe more, in some cases? When do we stop feeling alone and allow our spouses to comfort us, cover us and be just as committed to trusting God with us?

Trust God has partnered you with a man who is following His lead

The Word of God tells us, "But there is one thing I want you to know: The head of every man is Christ, the head of woman is man, and the head of Christ is God" (1 Corinthians 11:3, NLT). It's in the Word; there's no arguing it down, around or away. As much as we, as women, like to be in control, believe we run things, or, in some instances of flesh, we attempt to dominate our husbands, God has ordained them to be leaders over our homes. We have to trust that they are capable of hearing God's voice and using their relationship with Christ to keep us encouraged and supported on our own spiritual journeys. One of the resounding messages my husband would give me when I would vehemently question why he wasn't as pressed as I was about children was "I'm just trusting God." Now this should have been a wakeup call for me, but it usually just upset me. However, it should have convicted me to follow my husband's leadership and strengthen my trust in God and whatever His plan may be. If your husband does not have his own relationship to Christ and you find that he is not following God's leadership, pray about that, continue to be a spiritual example, and strive to show him unconditional love, in spite of spiritual shortcomings. This is something you would want to come into fruition before bringing a child into the world, into a home that is not equally yoked.

Communicate with your spouse

Hiding my desires from my husband made things significantly worse for me. I hid them because it got old real quick when I would express my desire for children and he would seem disinterested, unbothered, or would blatantly tell me he was waiting on God. We've already established that Brittney is stubborn, okay, so judge me as you wish, but I was not going to talk to someone about children who did not seem to empathize with me and the plight I was experiencing. Maybe your issue isn't children (though I would assume it is because you are reading this book), but as it pertains to communication with your spouse, you may struggle to be open and vulnerable in other places. It could be your job challenges, your feelings of purposelessness, your unspoken concerns with your lack of intimacy, issues with your platonic friends, literally anything. If you have ever experienced confiding in your husband about anything, and his response was not what you needed, it's likely you subconsciously swore to yourself you'd never bring this particular issue to him again.

The problem with that is, you should not be able to talk to any given person about anything so personal more than you can with your husband. I know, for the wives who feel like there are boundaries to pillow talk, this may not be for you. But as for me and my house, there are no barriers to communication. So for me to shut myself off was a big deal and one that resulted in bigger issues.

When I stopped sharing the highs and lows of my personal childless emotional rollercoaster, I began to believe that my husband should "just know" what I was going through. I expected him to be an empath and in tune with what he knew I had going on because I'd already told him ... but any wife who has been married for any length of time has likely heard their husband proclaim, "I'm not a mind reader." And my husband is the least of the mind readers, okay! If you don't tell him what you need outright, then you clearly don't need it. The lack of vulnerability led to animosity, disdain, and utter aggravation ... likely with myself, but ultimately it was taken out on him. Because I felt he was not emotionally connected to my needs, I distanced myself even more, to include mentally and physically, leading back to the lowered sex drive.

This didn't reconcile itself overnight. I had to first acknowledge what was happening, then make the journey to lessen the distance that I had placed between us. The biggest mistake we can make is assuming that our husbands don't care as much as we do, if at all, about this journey to conception. They do and are likely just coping in their own way. They could be wondering if it's their fault, especially if doctor's have confirmed that your reproductive system is overall healthy, or they could believe that the more they inquire about it, the worse it will make you feel. Men usually are naturally avoidant of conflict or emotional turmoil. They have not always been adequately taught how to deal with it and if we really reflect on our own experiences, neither have we, as women. Communication with your spouse will help alleviate that struggle.

Include your husband in your prayers

The most beautiful experience thus far on my personal journey has been inviting my husband to pray with me. Once the lines of communication were reopened, and we were aligned in our desires, praying over our unborn children was the most intimate event we could engage in. Chris placing his hand on my womb, his low, deep tone beseeching God on behalf of my heart's desires ... It was literally an experience that was one step of excitement below if we were to find out we were pregnant.

Beyond his covering of me, it was also my responsibility to cover him. One thing that he rarely shared with me - something I ultimately had to ask him outright - was that he was afraid that it wasn't me and that the issue lay with him. I found this to be the case after I had asked him for the fiftieth time to make an appointment with a urologist or to go to a fertility clinic to have his sperm health tested. He was always too busy, which wasn't a lie or cop out considering the intensity of his medical school studies at the time. It was basically a full-time, non-paying job. But in addition to that reality, he was concerned with learning negative results. Once I understood that, we were able to better align our prayers and communication regarding the imperativeness of knowing now versus later.

How often do you find yourself taking ownership of the possibility of infertility? Even if you have a diagnosis that says your body is the one that is challenged with conception, it is important to remember that God is working through *both* you and your husband. When you pray over your womb, pray for his as well ... his reproductive system that is. There are many men who just are not comfortable even considering that their bodies could be the presenting issue. Men rarely desire to seek a primary care physician when that regular everyday pain refuses to go away. Until he Is comfortable doing so, pray for his sperm, pray for their ability to move freely through your vaginal canal to meet your eggs. Pray for his willingness to attend to his physical health. Pray against anything that could be wrong with his reproductive system. Pray for his emotional stability and wellbeing. Ask God to show you how to support your husband in the way that matters most to him.

Remember the child you are praying for is *his* as well

You remember when I said that I had planned out my motherhood journey without my husband in mind. Okay, now remember even more that it *don't* work like that. You should not just be praying for your wants concerning your child. This is you and your spouse's seed to cover, protect and nourish together. Come together and pray over what you desire in your child – their qualities, their mental and physical capabilities, their purpose and call in Christ Jesus. Pray over yourselves as parents, that you remain in good standing with one another, united and strong under God's covenant. Pray for the qualities you know you each are challenged with maintaining that are essential for child rearing – patience, communication, empathy, inquisitiveness, exploration, love, kindness, gentleness, and the like. Pray that you both increase in your wisdom and understanding of who God has called you to be as parents so you can in turn pass that wisdom on to your offspring.

Pray for your child's wellbeing from the time he or she is conceived to the time they are born, and thereafter. I cannot tell you how often as a counseling intern that I have heard a couple or woman state they are concerned about bringing children into the world because of the chaotic ongoings of today's society. We have gotten so far from God that the idea of actually doing what He has called us to do, which is to be fruitful and multiply (Genesis 1:28), terrifies some of us into considerable disobedience. Pray now for your children's protection. Pray that they be able to go into the world, yet not be of it, and that if they do succumb to the wiles of the enemy that they find their way back to the Truth you will have instilled in them. Pray for them to be covered by the Spirit of our Living God, that they won't be harmed and that they will know what it means to seek the Heavenly Father when in trouble.

I keep a folder of prayers in the Notes app on my phone and some of them are prayers that I have found, specifically tailored to children. Occasionally, I will open the folder and read them as I continue to pray over my womb, my husband's sperm, and our future babies. This prayer is one of my favorites:

"Dear God, I pray for my future children that you will one day bless me with, Lord-willing. I pray that they would come to know you, Lord, surrender their entire life to you, and go share your good news with all others they come in contact with.

I pray that they would be missionaries for your kingdom. Make them servants with strong faith, hope, and love, representing you in all their deeds and actions. I pray that my future children would be warriors for you. May they declare your name with great boldness, confidence, and a humble heart.

God, I pray that they would share the gospel with their co-workers, friends, and family. I pray that the church community they are a part of would equip them with the tools and resources they need to share your salvation and saving

HANNAH'S PRAYER

grace with those who do not yet know your name.

As a future parent, I pray that you would equip me, God, to lead my children by example. When I'm in the grocery store, may I have the boldness to pray for the cashier. May I have the strength to show my children what a servant's heart is, like helping the elderly neighbor shovel her driveway. God, give me the strength to show your love to others when I am treated unfairly so that one day my children may do the same.

I pray that my future children would study your word each morning. Lord, may they pray to you in times of help and trouble, so they become missionaries for your kingdom's sake, whether that be locally or overseas.

In Jesus Name, Amen." (by Kelsey of *Good Point Grandma* blog)

Now, while I likely wouldn't shovel a neighbor's driveway and I don't always feel as bold in sharing my faith as I know my husband and I want our children to feel, this prayer exemplifies the type of faith, courage, and empathy we desire our children to have. You've heard the saying, "I want better for my children than I had" or some variation of that, and this prayer is that for us. So, join with your husband

and develop a prayer of your own (or search for one) that communicates to God exactly what you are hoping for with your divine conception.

REFLECTION

Spend some time with your husband, reflecting on what you desire for your conception, pregnancy, birth and eventual raising of your children. Jot those notes below and find scriptures that would remind you of God's promises or show your alignment with God's desire for your children as well. For example, *"We desire our children to be fearless and mentally strong"* (2 Timothy 1:7).

"'YOU ARE *blessed* BECAUSE YOU *believed* THAT THE *Lord* WOULD DO WHAT HE SAID.'"

LUKE 1:45 NLT

Check Your Circle

"So Peninnah would taunt Hannah and make fun of her because the Lord had kept her from having children. Year after year it was the same—Peninnah would taunt Hannah as they went to the Tabernacle. Each time, Hannah would be reduced to tears and would not even eat." 1 Samuel 1: 6-7 NLT

Whew! Okay, this is going to be the chapter for me because homegirl Peninnah could have caught all these hands, you hear me? It wasn't enough that Hannah could not have been Elkanah's only wife, she had to be belittled and degraded by the homewrecker as well. Yes, I know homewrecker probably isn't the proper term here, considering the times where having multiple wives was "appropriate." Let's be clear though, this is not by God's standards, but that's a dissertation for another day. I honestly can't get Elkanah's question out of my head here: "Am I not worth more than ten sons?" But yet, he's over here with more than one wife. I mean, is Hannah not worth more than the standard of having a harem of women around?

Let me digress because, if you can't tell, this part of the story is definitely a trigger for me.

The thing is, Hannah was married to Elkanah first. The tradition in these B.C. times was that if your first wife was unable to have children, then attaining a second one, who could, was perfectly permissible. Regardless of if the first wife could conceive or not, many men during these times, had multiple wives. The wealth and legacy that presumably came with many women and children Is something I still struggle with considering nowadays, more bodies to feed typically results in poverty. But those were the days nonetheless.

So back to the recount of Hannah being the first, and more preferred wife. She and Elkanah were married for about ten years according to the Midrash, which is a textual interpretation of biblical stories by Judaic authorities. And because she was unable to conceive, Elkanah was *compelled* to find another wife who could, therefore, Peninnah enters stage left. When I read the word "compelled," I immediately thought forced or pressured. It reminded me of how young men are often compelled by the fathers of young women to marry them after irresponsibly impregnating them. Ironic isn't it … At any rate, he marries Peninnah, but it's clear that it's just for her uterus, which absolutely sucks for her, so before I ransack her for being a complete witch to Hannah, I have to empathize with her plight.

To only be wanted for what you can give a man is never a good feeling. To be pulled into a polygamous relationship where the first wife is favored above you can't be pleasant to endure on a daily basis. I'm sure Peninnah didn't ask for this life though she may have been groomed for it – to marry and produce babies. Isn't that the same narrative we, as women, hear even now? So this feeling of being unworthy or unappreciated and even receiving less than, as Elkanah often gave Hannah a double portion of meat after his annual sacrifices, probably made Peninnah feel as though Hannah were teasing her, which likely led to jealousy. The Green-eyed Monster is no joke when uncontained and Peninnah fully succumbs to its power.

The Scriptures tell us that Peninnah taunted Hannah because she was barren. I can't specifically describe what this teasing looked like as the Word does not go that deep, but imagine, for a moment, that both women are tending to the home, cooking, cleaning, working, praying. Peninnah, watching Elkanah walk past Hannah and gently kiss her forehead, only to leave out of the front door, barely acknowledging her. Her seething turns into malicious taunting, and she calls one of her children into the room. She proceeds to coddle, hug, smother with kisses, and remark, "My child, *my child*, how blessed I am to have you and your siblings." Her eyes peering over at Hannah to see her content countenance diminish to sadness and depression at the reminder that the laughter and pitter patter of small feet don't belong to her own offspring. Peninnah devilishly grins, satisfied with the change in Hannah's demeanor and she then sends her child off, back to play with the other little ones, who's giggles, and melodies seem louder in Hannah's ears than before.

It's likely that this taunting could have been more overt, where Peninnah would blatantly call out Hannah's overwhelming truth or maybe there were arguments and choice words tossed her way. These are unknown details, but what we do know is that Hannah likely felt alone during this time. Her "sister wife" was, in her eyes, evil-spirited and apathetic to her plight and her husband wanted her to be simply satisfied with him. Her support was lacking.

It seems there are very few biblical accounts of barren women having an honorable community to lean on. There always seemed to be some ongoing competition between the primary wife and those that came along after, specifically for the task of birthing children that the first wife could not accomplish within a timely manner. The story of Abram, Sarai, and Hagar come to mind as one family that struggled like this. In this instance, Sarai encouraged Abram to sleep with Hagar because she hoped that her servant would birth a son that she could call her own, as in the case of a modern-day surrogate. But when Hagar became pregnant, she began to treat Sarai with contempt (Genesis 16:4), and with her husband's blessing, Sarai (whose name would soon be changed to Sarah) made Hagar's life a living hell to the point that the slave-girl ran away. Now if you read the entire story, Abram and Sarai's horrible decision to override God's plan for their lives ultimately results in the complicated split of the inheritance promised by God to Abram's (eventually Abraham) lineage. This is a reminder to trust God's timing and plan for your journey to motherhood. Moving too quickly or trying to do things on your own will only result in confusion or even delay in what God has promised you.

    Stories of barren women appear regularly throughout Scripture. You can consider those like Rachel and Leah, Rebekah, Samson's mother, Elizabeth, and so on. But only a few illustrate how support for such women made the journey somewhat easier. Elizabeth and Mary come to mind when I consider what a support system looks like while praying for your womb. While both Elizabeth and Mary were pregnant when they provided support for each other, it was the way in which that support was offered that aligns with the point of understanding who is in your circle as you navigate your mental, physical, emotional, and spiritual health and overall wellbeing during this time.

The disciple, Luke, illustrates Elizabeth's support of Mary in his recount of how John the Baptist's birth was foretold in the first chapter of his book of the Gospel. It starts with the story of Elizabeth's husband, Zachariah having an encounter with the angel, Gabriel, who tells him that he and his wife will bear a son, and name him John. Zachariah doesn't believe Gabriel, because like many of you reading this book, he felt he and his wife had exhausted all options and were beyond the capacity to conceive children. Because of his unbelief, Gabriel made Zachariah a mute for the duration of Elizabeth's pregnancy.

Sidebar: Stop doubting God! You never know what blessings you may be blocking when you walk in unbelief. While our God is gracious, He is also very adamant about us growing and developing our faith in Him so others may see it at work. When He places us in positions to be able to illustrate said faith and we fail that test, we leave others wondering what the point of trusting God is and ultimately tell God that His word is not enough for us. Don't wind up having your mouth shut because you have elected to walk in fear. Choose faith!

Now off my soapbox... Six months into Elizabeth's pregnancy, Gabriel then visited Mary and told her that as a young virgin who was about to get married, she would experience an immaculate conception and give birth to our Lord and Savior, Jesus Christ! Mary was terrified, concerned that her purity would be compromised and that she may be casted away. However, the Lord had His hands on her and the plan was already at work to leave her and her husband, Joseph, eternally in God's favor. Gabriel shared with Mary that not only would she conceive, but so would her cousin, Elizabeth. So days after this prophesy, Mary visited her cousin and experienced the following: *"[Mary] entered the house and greeted Elizabeth. At the sound of Mary's greeting, Elizabeth's child leaped within her, and Elizabeth was filled with the Holy Spirit. Elizabeth gave a glad cry and exclaimed to Mary, 'God has blessed you above all women, and your child is blessed. Why am I so honored, that the mother of my Lord should visit me? When I heard your greeting, the baby in my womb jumped for joy. You are blessed because you believed that the Lord would do what he said'"* (Luke 1: 39-45 NLT).

Mary needed Elizabeth to confirm what God had told her. No, she didn't go to her cousin's home to ask her about God's word; she was likely rushing over to simply see if she too had heard from the angel and was with child. But when she arrived, John jumped within his mother's belly and confirmed what Mary had been told. Elizabeth was able to affirm Mary and remind her that she was capable and equipped with what she needed to carry out the promises of God.

Who is in your circle? Are you surrounded by Peninnahs or Elizabeths? Are the people around you causing you to doubt the word of the Lord? Or are they leaping for joy and resounding faith with you? Are they laughing behind your back, or even in your face? Or are they praying and fasting with you?

A Peninnah may look like a relative commenting that your biological clock is ticking. Whether in ignorance or intentionality, this is far from supportive and affirming on such a sensitive journey. Peninnah may manifest itself as a concerned friend, telling you that maybe it just won't happen, and you should resolve to be okay with that or look into other options. As supportive as this may seem, if it negates what you *know* God has told you, then it's more passive aggressive or pessimistic than anything else. Peninnah might appear to be someone you don't even know, who is not directly taunting you, but causing you frustration. This could be another wife who announces a pregnancy, an unwed woman who seems to always pop out children, or even those annoying individuals who ignorantly post about what women should and should not do with their bodies, reproductive systems and desires concerning children. While it is not their intent to be a Peninnah, the influence of their words or actions in your life, may place them in that category.

What do you do with a Peninnah?

You keep her at a distance or completely disassociate from her. Yes, that may mean cutting off family or friends, or it could be as simple as setting boundaries. Let the naysayers know that you prefer they keep their negative comments to themselves. Tell your friend that though her words are coming from a sincere place, they aren't aligned with God's word as it was delivered to you. You pray for her. If she's pessimistic, that may be coming from a place of hurt, disappointment, personal trauma, or other negative experience. If she's someone who's life you seem to covet, consider that her journey to motherhood may have been just as, if not more, challenging, or that her life as a mother is not one that's most desirable.

I remember a conversation with my mom and sister, after finding out that a family member was pregnant with her fourth child. I asked them how it was that she, a single woman with other children out of wedlock, could be "blessed" to give birth to more babies, while I, as a married woman, continued to struggle to even have a pregnancy scare. Now, this was an issue within itself because I found myself in a judgmental position out of envy and disappointment. This person was not intending to be my Peninnah but that's how I perceived her because I believed her life as a mother was one I desired. In reality, it was absolutely not. I had to really re-examine my perspective on this situation. Did I really prefer to be a single mother to multiple children with more than one father to deal with? Or would I just wait on God to bless my husband and I in His perfect way? If you find yourself in such a position, pray for your envious spirit while also praying for that mother who may look at you and desire to swap lives in a Freaky Friday minute.

When it comes to an Elizabeth, this isn't just any and every person you encounter that says they'll be praying for you or drops an encouraging word in your spirit. An Elizabeth is a divine connection. It's one that can only be ordained by God, facilitated through prayer, and flourished through faith. Though Mary and Elizabeth were connected by blood, their prenatal relationship was a godly one, so much so that upon hearing Mary's voice, Elizabeth's baby leaped! Whose soul is jumping when you enter their presence? Whose presence is overwhelmed when your purpose is presented to them?

An Elizabeth looks like a prophetic word that God places in the heart of a distant friend, who only called to tell you what was in her spirit. Elizabeth is the prayer warrior that speaks your name, and you'd never know it unless asked. Elizabeth may manifest as a group of women who have been down this road and understand exactly what you are going through and can still remind you of God's promises.

If you ever feel alone on this journey, you will have to position yourself for community. This requires a few things:

1. Sharing your story.

I get it. There's often a stigma surrounding sharing your experiences with infertility or childlessness, but like with any other challenge, it's the only way to receive the support you need.

No one can help you if they don't know you need help. My community began to develop when people would ask how they could pray for me, and I would share that my husband and I were trying to conceive. I didn't immediately say I was experiencing infertility (I hadn't received that diagnosis anyway, so I did not want to label my waiting period), but people understood that we had been on this journey for a good length of time. Prayer requests turned into social media group requests and invitations, book recommendations and live prophesies. When I began writing this book, I shared that journey as well. It. Was. Not. Easy. ... but I did so because vulnerability is required for others to understand how they can support you.

Don't be afraid to share your journey. You don't have to broadcast it across Facebook, Instagram, or TikTok streets, but you should share with a trusted few, if nothing else. While your prayers are definitely enough, that of others would only magnify the impact and power of your request. Matthew 18:20 reminds us that where two or three are gathered, God is in the midst. I would venture to say this applies to prayers as well.

2. Identify what type of support you need.

All support may not be beneficial for you. Having someone constantly check in with you each month or asking about your "practicing" to conceive can be a bit much. It may be overwhelming to have a friend who is frequently sending you research articles or offering other insight as to what you could do to increase your chances of conception. You want to know what support looks like to you. If it's simply your support circle keeping you in their thoughts and prayers, then be clear about that.

Support may also vary from person to person. I had what I called my Hannah's tribe that consisted of approximately seven women. Only two of those women consistently heard my frustration and anger when it came to this experience. They were the only ones I felt most comfortable sharing that level of vulnerability with and I trusted them to listen and offer sound advice only if I needed to. They were the ones I would send late period updates to, even when I knew they probably would have just preferred I let them know when I had a positive test. They were also the only ones I would complain to when I saw pregnancy announcements. The rest of the tribe were supportive in their own rights. Some prayed, some offered fertility support and insight, and others simply shared their journeys to motherhood with me to give me hope. They were each exactly what I needed them to be when I needed them to be it.

3. Open yourself up to that support.

It's one thing to know you need support and even share your story to open the windows to receive it, but you must ensure you are ready for the support. This is a mental and emotional adjustment. Often when we are dealing with trauma, we easily shut down, close ourselves off to our emotions and to the voices of reason that attempt to pull us out of a steadily sinking hole. It can become worse when we feel like those who *should* support and encourage us, don't. We lock the box around our hearts even more securely.

Opening yourself up to support looks like understanding that you (1) need it, and (2) deserve it. You are not meant to go through challenges alone. The book of Hebrews 10:24 tells us we should "think of ways to motivate one another to acts of love and good works." Emotionally availing oneself of support is absolutely an act of love, love of yourself. Remembering that God promises you an abundant life and that even includes times of trouble. You are not meant to wallow in misery or depression; you are not meant to be alone and desolate with your trials. Opening your heart and

HANNAH'S PRAYER

mind to the encouragement that comes from a godly support system is one of the best things you can do for yourself during this time.

    A note: As you consider what support looks like for you and how to position yourself for receiving it, remain prayerful, asking God for the wisdom and discernment to filter through the noise that may disturb your mental or emotional wellbeing. Taking care of yourself is, above all else, the most important aspect of this journey. Your mind, body and spirit need to be at peace and if any level of support seems to disrupt that, it is perfectly okay to communicate that the support is no longer needed.

REFLECTION

Who is currently in your circle of support? If no one, brainstorm ways to connect with others. Lastly, identify what support looks like for you in this season/on this journey?

HANNAH'S PRAYER

"Standing on God's promises..."

It was one morning in worship that I was sitting prostrate and heard God say that He was healing me, and I felt stitching up of my uterus. In that moment, I knew all of the concerns, fears, and doubts of being able to conceive would not trump God's promises. As a woman that has dealt with PCOS and been told that I would have difficulty having children, this gave me hope.

As I have journeyed through the last 10 months of trying to conceive God has given me peace and told me that now is the time. The same doctor that diagnosed me with PCOS told me that I had enough eggs to fertilize, and they would put me on medication to get me to ovulate and not only would I have one, but two children and they would be 18 months apart. This was so prophetic as God has shown me a vision of a girl and boy that are very close in age, and I knew then that God was confirming through her that 2021 would be my year to conceive and that it would occur. Standing on God's promises.

– Crystal Corbin

"Sing, O childless woman, you who have never given birth! Break into loud and joyful *song*, O Jerusalem, you who have never been in labor. For the desolate woman now has *more children* than the woman who lives with her husband," says the Lord. "Enlarge your house; build an addition. Spread out your home and spare no expense! For you will soon be *bursting at the seams*. Your descendants will occupy other nations and resettle the ruined cities."

Isaiah 54:1-3 NLT

While You Wait

"And she made this vow: 'O Lord of Heaven's Armies, if you will look upon my sorrow and answer my prayer and give me a son, then I will give him back to you. He will be yours for his entire lifetime, and as a sign that he has been dedicated to the Lord, his hair will never be cut.'" 1 Samuel 1:11 NLT

Making your requests known to God takes a great deal of faith and courage, but even beyond that, we all understand that faith without works is dead (James 2:26). I spent a lot of time complaining versus truly praying in faith that God would meet my heart's desire. Many nights, I prayed and cried out to God in anguish, annoyed that another unmarried woman was announcing a pregnancy or frustrated that *He* had allowed my cycle to be weeks late to only have a negative pregnancy test and Aunt Flow showed up moments after enduring such disappointment. My prayers were not faithful. They were agitated and sometimes disrespectful.

In addition to that, my lifestyle was not conducive for children. I was at my unhealthiest weight due to work and school stressors, as I was eating and drinking anything and everything I craved. I was hardly sleeping or moving, and my emotional and mental attitude was not helping to alleviate the physical issues I was facing. It wasn't until I joined the Facebook support group I mentioned earlier, Supernatural Conception, Pregnancy & Birth, that I realized that all of my praying and crying meant nothing if I was not willing to adjust my daily habits to support my body in preparing for housing a child.

Hannah knew that it would take works, along with her faith to see her prayers fulfilled. Eli, the priest who had been at the temple while Hannah was praying, had to remind her of this. He initially believed her to be intoxicated and when she reassured him that she was not, and was only praying in great sorrow, he reminded her that she needed to remain that way and God would answer her prayers. When she left the temple, Hannah began to eat again (remember, she initially turned down her plate when Elkanah would give her a double portion), remained sober, and continued praying.

So, while waiting, it was important to actively pursue a healthy lifestyle. As a member of the Supernatural Conception, Pregnancy & Birth group, one of the moderators and a sister in

HANNAH'S PRAYER

my Hannah's tribe, Faith-Tomi Wilson, shared this vital and life changing information:

1. Stop any and all forms of birth control. This isn't just the pills or IUD or patch, this is also you having measures set that you have trusted more than GOD to get you pregnant... (Ex., tracking ovulation & it causing anxiety, worry or fear)
2. Start a prenatal ASAP!
3. BEGIN a 21-day detox, fast or just really clean eating with an emphasis on fruits, veggies, lean proteins and tons of water! The focus is developing a HEALTHY lifestyle & communing with the Lord.
4. Walk/exercise/be active 3-5x a week for 30 mins or more. BREAK A SWEAT!
5. Start speaking/praying to your child(ren) in your womb as if you are pregnant already.

When I initially saw the post, I'm almost certain I rolled my eyes because I was not in the right frame of mind to "adjust" my lifestyle. I had gotten comfortable with my weight gain, I was definitely enjoying the weekend turn-up and felt as if I didn't have much time to move my body due to my schedule. I also simply believed, *It shouldn't take alla dat!* My mental focus at the time was sustaining my sanity and what I was doing was working for me, but it was not allowing me to achieve the goal of conception.

I can't recall when the turning point came, but I do believe it was around the moment where my husband and I were receiving prayer from my grandfather about this very issue, and I heard the Lord give me a command to follow these guidelines if I wanted to see my prayers answered. His command was much more specific, but for the purpose of this book's message, I understood that He required me to do all of these things. So I did. Yes, I ran into some setbacks and challenges, but overall, I lost the weight, began to eat and sleep better, and concentrated on speaking the Word of the Lord over my womb while also putting my faith into action. What does putting faith into action look like for you as you wait for God to fulfill His Word? What habits or behaviors do you need to start, stop or change? Consider the following:

Work while you wait.

As Faith mentioned in her group post, you have to do the work. There's no way you can conceive if you have any conception control methods in place. Whether it be the pill, an IUD, or even a natural withdrawal process, you have to stop it. I know this is challenging for my sisters who face issues such as PCOS and take cycle regulating medication. I won't encourage you to stop anything that your doctor has prescribed for you but have this conversation with him or her and inquire as to how you can ensure you are not preventing pregnancy with any hormone balancing drugs. If your spouse has been adamant about withdrawal, go back to the chapter on communicating with your husband to determine if you all are on the same page or not. Nothing can progress if you all are not. Don't resort to tricks and games to get what you want. God will not bless that.

Begin to take care of yourself. That means eating, sleeping and taking the appropriate supplements. I started taking prenatals a year before I did anything else that would have benefited my body. Those along with other supplements, such as Maca root were recommended by my prenatal midwife to include in my health regime. Again, talk to your doctor to see what's helpful for you and please monitor how your body responds to anything new you may intake.

Work out your body in a way that works for you. You don't have to start doing CrossFit or extreme bootcamp to get healthy, and you certainly don't have to neglect your favorite foods, but everything in moderation. Walk (indoors or outside) for 20-30 minutes a day. Search feasible workout videos on YouTube. Couple that with a balanced and healthy diet. Research meal plans for your blood type, monitor your ingestion of processed foods, and try to eat as clean as possible, with the occasional cheat meal every now and then. If you plan out your health regime, you will likely stick to it, so write down what you desire to do and how you plan to do it. Schedule it in your calendar just as you would any other meeting, appointment or task. Do the work!

    Work also looks like being purposeful in your daily walk with Christ and life. One of the biggest mistakes I made was proclaiming that I would give up everything God had given me for a child. I said it often, loud and proud ... The thing about it was, all those other things I was willing to toss aside were a part of my divine purpose and calling in Jesus Christ. Yeah, probably a huge slap in His face. Just like when Elkanah felt that he wasn't enough for Hannah, I'm sure this made God feel like He was not enough for me. And I honestly couldn't even lie and say that in those moments He, or anyone else or thing I presently possessed, was. It was as if without children, my life was meaningless, and that was a lie from the devil that I demonstrated proudly in my daily actions.

HANNAH'S PRAYER

When I think of what it looks like to pursue purpose while waiting for God to bless you, I think of Ruth from the Bible. Ruth had lost everything but followed her mother-in-law to a foreign land where she immediately began to work. She knew God called her to be faithful to Naomi, her family and their spiritual practices. "But Ruth replied, 'Don't ask me to leave you and turn back. Wherever you go, I will go; wherever you live, I will live. Your people will be my people, and your God will be my God.'" (Ruth 1:16 NLT). While it was clear that it was a desire to remarry, it was not so overwhelming that Ruth allowed it to overpower her willingness to follow God's plan. She had no idea what lay ahead in this new land and finding a husband may have not been the priority on her list. She wanted to honor the woman of God who had impacted her life.

A lot of theologians suggest that Ruth worked while waiting for Boaz, but that's not what the scripture suggests.

> *"One day Ruth the Moabite said to Naomi, 'Let me go out into the harvest fields to pick up the stalks of grain left behind by anyone who is kind enough to let me do it.' Naomi replied, 'All right, my daughter, go ahead.' So Ruth went out to gather grain behind*

> *the harvesters. And as it happened, she found herself working in a field that belonged to Boaz, the relative of her father-in-law, Elimelech.* **Then** *Boaz asked his foreman, 'Who is that young woman over there? Who does she belong to?' And the foreman replied, 'She is the young woman from Moab who came back with Naomi. She asked me this morning if she could gather grain behind the harvesters. She has been hard at work ever since, except for a few minutes' rest in the shelter.'"* (Ruth 2:2-3, 5-7 NLT)

Ruth saw that work needed to be done and while she was hard and work, *Boaz spotted her*, not the other way around. She was not working to be seen or sought after. She worked because it was her calling and purpose in that season. As a result of her being in position, she was able to receive a blessing in the form of a husband, contributing to the lineage that eventually birthed our Christ Jesus.

Are you in position? Are you working? Or have you neglected your purpose because of the pain you are experiencing while waiting for

God to answer your prayers. One of the more harmful actions we can take on our spiritual journey is to pray to God for something and not do as He asks us in other aspects of life. If He has called you to start a business, organization or program, and you're walking in fear regarding doing so, or you simply just aren't feeling the assignment, how is it that you anticipate Him blessing you by meeting your request? I truly believe that God gives us opportunities to show ourselves approved and part of that can be manifested in the work He has called us to do in this world for the building of His Kingdom. If I say "no," to His request, why should I expect a "yes" from Him regarding mine? I don't believe our God is down with the tit-for-tat lifestyle, but we have to be realistic in assuming that it may be a lot more difficult for Him to answer our prayers in a way we desire if we are not responding to Him in the same manner. Work while you wait.

Engage in praise.

If you aren't praising God in the midst of any storm, you're doing it wrong. There are little to no stories in the Bible that suggest that any person waiting for God to restore, renew, revive, or respond sat in depression until the prayer was answered. In any situation, you praise your way through. You praise like it's already done because that is what faith requires. You also praise when it happens for others because if God can do it for them, He can do it for you as well.

I know Job is probably the overly used example for this, but rightfully so. There is no one on earth, even today, who I can call on to compare to the loss Job endured. While I'm sure there are many, especially across the seas, who I may never meet, Job is one who is the perfect example of what it means to praise through pain. Job lost everything (family, friends, and his health) and yet he still honored God, even when others told him to forsake God since it seemed God had forsaken Him.

> "Job stood up and tore his robe in grief. Then he shaved his head and fell to the ground to worship. He said, 'I came naked from my mother's womb, and I will be naked when I leave. The Lord gave me what I had, and the Lord has taken it away. Praise the name of the Lord!'" (Job 1:20-21 NLT)

Job understood that without God nothing else mattered, so he would not dare position anything above his Heavenly Father. This has to be our posture and attitude during this time. We praise God for what He *has* done for us because as cliché as the saying, "If he doesn't do anything else, He's done enough" is, it's the truth. We are given grace each and every day that we open our eyes and take a breath. While God desires to give us much more than that, we are not deserving of it and should not behave as if we are. It should be with humility that we praise and honor Him while we wait for His answer, and even if His answer is not what we desire, our praise must be greater, knowing that His ways are higher and better than our own.

Prepare as if it's already done.

In Faith's Facebook group post, my sister's last tip focused on behaving as if the prayer is already answered. She said to begin to pray over your womb and speak to your children as if you are already pregnant. Now, this can be emotionally triggering for some, but if you have done everything else up until this point, your faith should be limitless. Name your children, so when you pray you can call on them directly. Touch your belly, anoint it with oil, and ask your husband to pray over your womb, his reproductive system, and your future seed. Purchase small baby items as tokens of faith. This was something my mother-in-law recommended, and I found myself in the baby department of Walmart, buying a couple of pacifiers. Since then, I have received a baby thermometer, onesie and stuffed animal...all from other loved ones who also believe in God's promises over my life. These items symbolize a faith-based preparation that God will fulfill His Word. Don't avoid this step out of fear but pursue it with great and bold belief that God is going to do what He has said.

This is also a great opportunity to pray for your preparation. Children thrive in environments that are suitable for them, so if your home, your marriage, or your emotional capacity is not quite there yet, pray for opportunities to better it. Looking into improving your financial stewardship is one way to prepare for the monetary obligations that come with children. Understanding how your spending habits may need to change or educating yourself on what savings opportunities there are for your children's future are also great ways to prepare for the manifestation of God's promises.

Do you and your spouse struggle with communicating with one another? Are you often fighting without realizing it? How emotionally constant are each of you? All of these are behaviors children will witness and learn from. This time of preparation should also focus on discovering and improving behaviors you would want your children to emulate. This may look like going to counseling or spending time in prayer, asking for wisdom in approaching and interacting with your spouse, so that you can, in turn, practice those same habits with your children. Don't sit and twiddle your thumbs, as my grandmother would say. Prepare as if what you have asked for is in the works or already done, so you are not surprised or forced into major changes when the time does come.

REFLECTION

What work do you need to be doing as you wait for God's response to your prayers for children? Name areas of concern and highlight scriptures to directly address them. Then take them to God in prayer.

Praise the Lord!
Yes, give *praise*, O servants of the Lord.
Praise the name of the Lord!
Blessed be the name of the Lord
now and forever.
Everywhere—from east to west—
praise the name of the *Lord*.
For the Lord is high above the nations;
his glory is higher than the heavens.
Who can be compared with the Lord our God,
who is *enthroned* on high?
He stoops to look down
on heaven and on earth.
He lifts the poor from the dust
and the needy from the garbage dump.
He sets them among *princes*,
even the princes of his own people!
He gives the childless woman a *family*,
making her a *happy mother*.
Praise the Lord!

Psalm 113

When It Happens

"For this child I prayed, and the Lord has granted me my petition that I made to him."

1 Samuel 1: 27 ESV

    At the time of finishing this book, I will have been six weeks pregnant. Tears flood my eyes at even writing those words because never in a million years did I believe God would answer my prayer before I completed this task. And now that I think about it, this is my first real cry of gratefulness since finding out I was pregnant a little over a week prior to this chapter being written. I have been in utter shock for the most part, while also dealing with some physical symptoms of this new phase of life. It's still hard to believe, but I know that everything I have done up until this point has been out of pure obedience. Even with the changes and adjustments I struggled with the most, I tried to comply to His will with a good and clean heart.

    Now is the time to plan for victory! Now is the time to set your mind on what you know will be yours! God has great plans for you and motherhood shall be a part of that, in accordance to His Will. That last part is the clause we have to be willing to accept. Maybe you won't give birth naturally or without medical assistance, but you must know and accept that God's will for your journey to motherhood is beyond you. It's to bring forth an immutable testimony that will encourage others to faithfully pursue Him.

So whenever and however it happens for you, you must be willing to continue to praise God, remain in a posture of prayer, and trust in Him. These practices don't end just because you have received a positive pregnancy test, the facility treatment worked, or the adoption was approved. The work is just beginning at those points. You are now responsible for continuing your spiritual growth so that your child can glean and grow from it as well. In addition to that, your story is now a gateway for souls to be saved and for those who have lacked in their faith walk to be revived!

Do you remember when John the Baptist leaped in Elizabeth's stomach upon being in the presence of Mary, who was pregnant with Jesus? That's the impact your story will have on every person who hears it, and you want to be ready and willing to walk diligently in that distinguished purpose. So when you receive what you have been praying for, position yourself to:

Praise and rejoice

Do not stop praising God, as a matter of fact, now is the time to praise Him more for answering your prayer. When I found out I was pregnant, I honestly was in such shock that I don't think my first words were to thank or praise God. For some odd reason, I called my mom (at 4am) and cried in what felt like confusion and despair. I couldn't tell you why if I wanted to. Yes, I was happy, but I was also a little afraid and nervous that it wasn't true. I took three tests back-to-back, and they were loud and clear, but for some reason, I felt like it wasn't my reality. In spite of that brief and weird moment, I did take time to thank God.

I sat up for the next two hours, disregarding the fact that I had to go to work within the next four, and prayed. I prayed and told God how thankful I was for Him giving me what I had asked for. I thanked Him for trusting me with this gift. I praised Him for being a Jehovah Jireh, my provider, of all of my needs and those wants that aligned with His will and purpose for my life. I was grateful and you should be as well. No matter how long it may take to get there or the route the journey takes to get to the destination. The fact remains that none of us are deserving, but through God's compassion and grace for His people, we are blessed to carry *His* children.

Continually pray

This is also not the time to stop praying. As soon as I saw the positive pregnancy test, that cry of despair gave way to anxiety. Was I really ready for this? I had let it go and though it wasn't a forgotten prayer, it was one I had resolved God wasn't ready to reward me with. Why now? What should I do next? What happens if I miscarry? God wouldn't give me this child to simply take it away, would He?

There were so many negative thoughts that swirled through my mind before a solid positive one stuck. This is simply a trick and tactic of the enemy and you have to be prepared to ward it off. Luckily, I had my mother on the phone with me at the time to calm me down ... at 4am (I love you, mama!), but had she not been there, I would have needed to be equipped with the full armor of God because the way these thoughts attacked me, I would have lost without some level of spiritual protection.

When you find out that God has answered your birthing prayers, keep praying. The Bible does command us to pray without ceasing and to give thanks in all situations (1Thessalonians 5:17-18), and just as we should continue to rejoice when a prayer is answered, we should keep on praying in the same vein. Praying will keep us humble and position us to receive all that comes with this "yes" God has given us. It maintains a level of spiritual clarity necessary to ward off demonic attacks and spiritual wavering.

Just as you prayed to prepare for this moment, you can now begin to pray for your transition into motherhood, whether it be your actual pregnancy or the process of bringing a child from another environment into your home. Pray for God to cover you and your child as your body changes. Read *Supernatural Childbirth* by Jackie Mize and prepare to evade the woes of pregnancy, labor, and delivery. Pray for effective resources to help you in raising and caring for your child. Pray for your child's mental and emotional wellbeing. Just pray! Because if you believed you were being attacked by the enemy on the journey to give birth or have a child, you truly want to be prepared against the wiles of the enemy now that you are guiding another one of God's children to be a vessel for the kingdom.

Maintain healthy practices

Just as you prepared your body to be an incubator for another human, you are going to need to maintain that level of health and wellness throughout your pregnancy and into your time as a mother, chasing after or trying to keep up with your children. Yes, I know...what about the cravings? Let me tell you, I have not eaten so many carbs in months, but in the first seven days of knowing I was pregnant, my carb intake skyrocketed from about 20% to 60%. I felt disgusted, but I also knew I had to give myself grace and reflect on if my "cravings" were more mental than they were anything else. Now, don't get me to lying because if you asked me if I had three hotdogs for lunch and a footlong sub sandwich for dinner a few nights ago, I would have to plead the fifth. But if you also asked me how I am maintaining my health, I could say that I still workout 3-5 times a week and try to eat only when I'm hungry (because these carb cravings ain't going nowhere).

Maintaining healthy practices means doing what fits your new lifestyle. For me, eating six small meals a day and doing a sixty-minute cardio-intensive workout wasn't working well anymore. I was exhausted, lying in bed for hours at a time, which prevented me from doing things like meal prepping. I was cramping nonstop, which I'll dive into in the next session, but the pain and anxiety that came with it resulted in more lying around. And the nausea wasn't conducive for jumping around and high stepping on cinder blocks during my brick workout that I would normally engage in. Some of the healthy things I was doing just a few days earlier were now counterproductive to the things my body needed like rest and a few additional calories to support my changing body. I'm not saying I will go the entire pregnancy skipping workouts and creating excuses for ordering pizza but listening to my body and adjusting as necessary will be a priority.

As in anything health-related, consult your doctor. Do your research and find out what workouts are best for you, what you should or should not be eating (I'm so sad about not being able to have sushi for the next eight months), and ensure your body is getting what it needs. If nothing else, increase your fruit, veggie and water intake and find a good prenatal vitamin to carry you through your third trimester and beyond. Remembering that your body is a temple above all else (1 Corinthians 6:19).

Keep your faith in God

Earlier, I mentioned having a great deal of anxiety around the cramps I experienced the first week after receiving a positive pregnancy result. My body has changed a great deal as I transitioned from my twenties and began to take supplements to assist in natural fertility increase. One of those changes included premenstrual cramps. Fortunately for me, growing up, that was not one of my monthly issues. When Aunt Flo showed up, she just showed up. I wouldn't know until I could feel that I needed to put on a pad or insert a tampon. It was a blessing and a curse because I evaded the annoyance of such pain as cramps, but I could easily have a public blood show incident before making it to a restroom.

Well after I started taking prenatals, Maca root, and another ovulation regulator, I started having premenstrual cramps days before my cycle would arrive. I hated it! I was perfectly fine before with Ruby's pop up, but nonetheless, this was my new normal. The issues arose when my cycles then became irregular. Well not irregular, but what was normally and predictably a 28-day cycle, sometimes would delay a week or two. This delay would cause emotional turmoil because I would believe I was pregnant, take a test, and it would be negative; then literally moments later, my cycle would begin. It was a tumultuous headache.

At any rate, this recurring cycle caused fear and anxiety to show itself the week I found out I was pregnant because my cramps were unable to be suppressed. Though the certified nurse midwife I saw as my primary prenatal care professional assured me these experiences were normal, I could only think that at some point Flo would come bursting through, killing my dreams. Miscarriage was all I could hear each time my stomach knotted and churned.

After sharing the episodes with a couple of ladies in my Hannah's tribe, they got me together real quick. "Aht! Aht! Positive energy only please!" and "Stay off GOOGLE! It will have you worried! You prayed for this child and God provided. He will see you through!" I had been on Google and my sisters were right. Why would God make good on His promise only to allow me to experience an immediate loss? That was not going to be my portion.

Instead of focusing on negative thoughts such as this one, I chose to hold fast to my faith. God has answered my prayer, and while I know so many have experienced miscarriage or other laborious issues, it is my choice to hold God to His promise and maintain my faith in His Word. This requires that I stay in the Word ... and off Google, while also affirming myself, my body, and my baby on this journey.

A few affirmations I have spoken over myself are:

- I will carry this baby to full-term.
- My body is healthy and whole.
- My baby will be mentally, emotionally, and physically well.

- I will not succumb to the woes of pregnancy (e.g. morning sickness).
- I will give birth, naturally, to a healthy baby.

In addition to affirming myself and speaking the Word over my life, I also opted to not function in fear. Often women do not share their pregnancy announcements until after the first trimester to ensure that they've passed that sensitive timeframe where a miscarriage is more probable. Because I was already having that fear, I chose to use the announcement as a move of faith and share with a select number of people that we were expecting. I chose to do this because not doing it, for me, would mean that I'm feeding a fear and allowing it to control and overpower my faith. Some would not agree with that and simply call it a precaution ... and that's fine. For me, it was a courageous move to let God know, I trust Him and am holding Him to carrying us through this pregnancy completely.

Whatever maintaining your faith looks like for you, pursue that wholeheartedly. There are many obstacles you may face, mentally and physically, as you journey through the process of becoming a mother. Equipping yourself with the necessary spiritual warfare will be imperative. Going into this next phase of womanhood cannot be taken lightly. Remember, you are carrying purpose. You are birthing greatness. You are taking on a kingdom responsibility greater than yourself and you must be prepared. Someone great said, "Stay ready and you never have to get ready." Don't slack off now. Praise God and thank Him for answering this prayer and begin praying the next ... and the next ... and the next. A mother's prayer never ceases.

Remember Hannah's vow

Hannah vowed to dedicate her son back to God (1 Samuel 1:11). She knew that her child would be a gift from the Lord and that God would be lending this gift to her to care for with an understanding that Samuel would be used for God's purpose and mission. Keep this in mind. You are asking God to bless you, and in turn, you must be willing to allow God to use your child in whatever way He chooses. In Hannah's case, she was urged to allow Samuel to live with the priest, Eli, to be mentored for the call God had placed on his life. She had to essentially give him up when he was just a few years old.

Are you willing to truly dedicate your child to Christ? This is beyond the traditional christening, such a beautiful ceremony with deeply rooted spiritual meaning... This is doing with your child whatever God requires of you. It could be as extreme as sending him or her off for spiritual mentorship or something simple, yet still sacrificial, like placing your child in a particular school, moving to ensure the environment he or she is growing up in is beneficial, or even you, as a parent, changing your career or educational path to better support your child's development. Whatever the "ask" is, it should be your heart's posture to remember the vow(s) you may have made during your praying season and keep them sacred.

Share your testimony

If you have already shared your struggles, it's now time to share the successes. While you don't have to make a Facebook or Instagram post the day you receive your positive news, at some point, you do want to share the good news. Sharing is not just for you to receive congratulatory words and affirming comments. You are sharing a testimony. The goal here is to reach hearts and save souls. Your sharing should intentionally encourage those who are watching, reading or listening to turn their faith back to God and to lean on Him, even when the situation seems bleak.

I've seen stories of women who have experienced loss, infertility, conception challenges, etc. share their triumph in the end in various ways. An acquaintance of mine posted a 2-hour video about her rainbow baby, where she sat with her husband and discussed how they had lost their first and kept the second a secret all the way up to his birth for the sake of their emotional wellbeing. Faith, from the Supernatural Conception, Pregnancy & Birth group, conducted a series on her prenatal and postpartum experience, offering spiritual insight, holistic tips, and bringing in experts to help educate women across the world. Another social media connection recently shared the testimony of how God answered her prayers of giving birth after being told that she would have slim chances of doing so by doctors.

It doesn't matter when or how you elect to share, but God calls us to proudly share our stories with all the nations, not for personal praise but for His glory. In Luke 8:39 Jesus gave a command to the man he healed from a demonic attack, and he told him to "go home and declare what God has done for you." 1 Chronicles 16:8 encourages us to make the Lord's deeds known to others. Psalm 107:2 reminds us that the redeemed of the Lord must say so. When you have been redeemed of suffering, of challenges, of hardship...let everyone know what God has done for you. It's easy for us to complain when we don't have what we desire. We find it a bit

HANNAH'S PRAYER

easier to tell everyone how we feel God has forgotten us or that we feel He is not near, but what do we do when all of that proves itself to be a lie? Just as somberly as we shared our woes, we should eagerly share our wins through Christ Jesus. Don't hold back your testimony because it is sure to help someone else. I know that through my obedience, I have done just that.

REFLECTION

Plan your praise. Thank God in advance. Write your story right now. What will you do *when it happens?*

HANNAH'S PRAYER

"God has given us His word..."

For many years I had convinced myself that I wasn't able to have children after trying for 12 plus years. After graduating high school, I became pregnant and was pressured into having an abortion that my mom persuaded was in my best interest living under her roof. I didn't take the time to grieve or feel what I felt. Over time, I had lost my voice, my power, and the ability to dream again.

Years later, every day was a constant battle, not knowing how to pray and fix my mouth to ask God when I would become a mother. When will it be my turn? It made me bitter and emotionally unstable. Then one night in fall 2020 I did something amazing. I found the courage to pray boldly without guilt nor fear and ask God for my baby. He confirmed my prayer within days through a dream. I received His YES!! It was time. I was prophesied weeks later that I would conceive before the year is out and I would birth a prophet. Then I was added to the Supernatural Conception group on Facebook. November 28, 2020. I randomly took a test, and it was positive. My husband and I were pregnant. God had given us His word and promises. It is only by His divine timing that we receive in the natural what's already ours in the Spirit.

– Keila Boyd

It will be like a woman suffering the pains of *labor*. When her child is born, her anguish gives way to *joy* because she has brought a new *baby* into the world.

John 16:21 NLT

Afterword

It is my sincerest hope that this book has brought you what you need in this time of challenge and trial. Whether you are praying for a child, have lost a child, or are in the process of taking in a child that is not naturally born of you, it is important to know that you are not alone. Conversations around infertility and reproductive health are steadily occurring across various media and I encourage you to be a part of those discussions, in a way that proves to be healthy for you. Sitting and suffering in silence will not work. Use these platforms as an opportunity to increase your knowledge and understanding, grow your faith, and surround yourself with supportive individuals.

This book was written out of obedience. I never intended for this to be a story I would share, and that would be around for many years to come, even after I have had children. However, I also did not understand how much a story such as this one was needed. When I began sharing bits and pieces of it on social media, viewers mostly saw and encouraged my vulnerability, but many others sent me private messages that let me know I was helping them with my story. I truly

HANNAH'S PRAYER

believe my obedience and willingness to share prompted God to reward me with my first child during this process. And while I am nowhere near a delivery date, I dedicate my child back to Him even now, because I know that he or she is nothing less than a gift.

Keep your faith strong. Fight for your heavenly rights. Ward off attacks of the enemy. Watch your eye and ear gates. Fill your heart and mind with positive, spiritually enriching material. Take care of yourself. God has not forgotten you. Your Hannah's prayer will be answered. Prepare yourself for whatever that looks like when the time comes and praise God in advance.

Thank you for reading. Please feel free to send prayer requests, share your testimonies, or other comments and feedback to me at contact@brittneyholmesjackson.com.

Reader Discussion Questions

1. What has been your greatest struggle with this journey? If you are not the one journeying to motherhood, who are you supporting and what has been a challenge in doing so?

2. When you consider praying specifically about anything, what would you consider to be best practices in doing so?

3. Has your spiritual walk suffered due to loss or unanswered prayers? If so, how? What from this reading could you use to restore your faith?

4. This book focused on the story of Hannah, but also included anecdotes from the lives of Sarah, Hagar, Ruth, Elizabeth and Mary. Which of these women do you mostly relate to and why? What from her story can you apply in your own life?

5. If not for a child, what are you currently praying for? What are you doing to prepare for receiving that answered prayer?

6. What signals occur when your prayer life is beginning to grow inconsistent? Create a plan for reconvening with Christ.

HANNAH'S PRAYER

7. When you consider having a Hannah's tribe, it can be for the purpose of supporting any prayer you are currently focused on. Who would you consider to be a part of your Hannah's tribe and why?

8. Do you find it difficult to maintain communication with your spouse/partner in troubling times? What does that feel like for you? What, if any, insight from this book resonated with you to prevent that from happening?

9. How are you currently sharing your story? Do you struggle with being fully vulnerable? What parts of your story are you hesitant to share?

10. What are you fully expecting God to do in your life, as a mother or otherwise? State or write a declaration and remain faithful to God and trust in His timing.

www.ingramcontent.com/pod-product-compliance
Lightning Source LLC
Chambersburg PA
CBHW070921080526
44589CB00013B/1388